Victory in the Valley
(A Christian Approach to Grief)

A Series of Sermons by
Rev. Bob Marcaurelle

ISBN 979-8-89428-439-2 (paperback)
ISBN 979-8-89428-440-8 (digital)

Copyright © 2024 by Rev. Bob Marcaurelle

All rights reserved. No part of this publication may be reproduced, distributed, or transmitted in any form or by any means, including photocopying, recording, or other electronic or mechanical methods without the prior written permission of the publisher. For permission requests, solicit the publisher via the address below.

Christian Faith Publishing
832 Park Avenue
Meadville, PA 16335
www.christianfaithpublishing.com

Printed in the United States of America

To Frank and Pearl Myers (Anderson, South Carolina) who, because of their generosity, *Victory in the Valley* was first published.

When I first preached these series of sermons, a dedicated layman in our church said he would pay for them to be printed if I would give them out in the grief ministry of our church and to anyone else who requested. His name was Frank Myers, and he is now with the Lord in heaven. Since that time, several laymen and women have graciously and generously and voluntarily provided the funds for reprinting. To all of them, this little book is dedicated (January 2001).

CONTENTS

1. Victory in the Valley 1
2. The Defeat of Death 14
3. Joy Right Now in the New Jerusalem 27
4. The Hope of Heaven 38
5. For Those with No Miracle 52

CHAPTER 1
Victory in the Valley
(Psalm 23:4)

The pain of bereavement, which we call grief, is the price we pay for love. In fact, the more the love, the more the hurt. The closer we are, the deeper the wound when we are torn apart.

Grief is so painful, and the loneliness is so unbearable that we often envy our departed loved one. The peace of death seems far better than the pain of being left behind.

Grief is a universal experience. We spend our lives gathering around us those things and especially those people that really matter and make life worthwhile. When we lose them, grief sets in. Grief is an important, normal, potentially helpful, and potentially harmful response to loss. Grief can make or break us.

The deepest grief, of course, is over the loss of our loved ones. If this has happened to you, then you know the emptiness, the loneliness, and the almost unbearable pain that comes to those who walk in this valley. This is not just another in the list of life's blows; this is the blow that threatens our very existence or sanity. As Edgar Jackson says, "The pattern of our days is shattered beyond recall." This is an amputation. This is a fact about which we can do nothing. All our tears, prayers, and piety cannot erase the verdict: "He is gone! He is dead! He is not coming back!"

When death rudely invades our comfortable lives, we as Christians do not know how to act. We are torn by conflicting emotions. We have faith that God cares, but we are tortured by doubts about why He allowed this terrible hurt to come our way.

We rejoice that our loved one has gone to be with the Lord, but our sorrow over our loss is almost unbearable. Like most who have lived on this planet, we are walking through what David called "the valley of the shadow of death" (Ps. 23:4). Others, we know, have been here; but we feel like the first one and the only one to ever hurt like this.

This experience has the power to crush the life right out of us. The old saying is true: "In bereavement, it is often the survivor who dies." We have all known people in grief who have drawn into a shell and moved from living to merely existing. They are a burden to themselves and everyone around them. On the other hand, there are those who grieve deeply; keep their mental and spiritual balance; and go on to live richer, fuller lives.

A good example of this is Catherine Marshall. After losing her husband, Peter, in the prime of his life, she picked up the pieces, became a devotional writer, and has ministered to untold millions who have followed her into the valley.

The message of Christianity for this awful hour is that we can have such victory. The Bible says, "All things work together" for our good (Rom. 8:28). Even grief can work for our good and the good of others. The big question, of course, is "How? How can we find victory in the 'valley of death's dark shadow' (Ps. 23:4)?"

I. You Must Face the Fact of Grief

Grief, the pain you now feel, is the universal and the normal reaction to the irrevocable loss of someone we love. It is natural and necessary, but we have two huge obstacles that keep us from accepting it and expressing it and ultimately conquering it.

One obstacle is the fact that we are Americans. In our Western culture, we are spoiled. We are not conditioned to face anything unpleasant or painful. Our goal and our god is happiness. Death is an embarrassment. We make our corpses as lifelike as possible, bury them as soon as possible, and hurry back to our way of life.

in our society," says Gary Collins, "we have encouraged ourselves to deny death and to respond to the bereavement of others with little more than a card or casserole or...some cut flowers."[1] Mourners are pressured to keep their faith, keep their composure, and snap out of their grief as soon as possible.

There is extra pressure if we are Christians. We put pressure on ourselves to keep up our image of being "good" Christians. With a thousand doubts screaming to be heard, we deny our grief, smile, and calmly say, "God never makes a mistake." If in an unguarded moment, a word of doubt sneaks to the surface, we usually have a Christian friend ready to say, "You know God never makes a mistake." Thus, our true feelings are buried and denied because they are not in keeping with our concept of a good Christian.

Now it is certainly true that God never makes a mistake. But it is not true that good Christians will always *feel* that He never makes a mistake. When our lives tumble in, we will feel things like pain, bitterness, anger, fear, frustration and depression.

Such feelings must be honestly admitted and openly dealt with or they will surface in harmful, pathological, damaging ways. We must face the fact that grief explodes into our lives and hurts us in a thousand places and a thousand different ways.

We must remember that grief is a universal experience. We have not been singled out for special hurt. Ever since Adam and Eve wept over the grave of Abel, members of Adam's race have stood over lonely graves and wept. Death is one fact of life we must accept. Longfellow put it well:

> There is no flock, however watched and tended,
> But one dead lamb is there!
> There is no fireside, howsoe'er defended,
> But has one vacant chair!

II. You Must Face the Facts of Grief

You have looked at this dark, lonesome valley called grief. If you love anyone, you cannot avoid it. Now we are going to walk through the valley and look at the various facets or stages of grief. There seems to be a predictable pattern.

There are distinct stages through which we pass, each with its dangers and with its opportunities for growth. There is a wealth of material on this subject. I highly recommend the little book *Good Grief* by Granger E. Westberg.

In discussing these stages, we must not make the mistake of stereotyping everyone and squeezing them into one mold. We differ as persons, and we will differ in our experiences of grief. Your stages of grief may come in the opposite order from mine. You may not even feel an emotion, like anger at God that wipes another person out. Some may have all these symptoms and some only a few. The most prevalent reactions are crying, depression, and restlessness.

We cannot wrap all these stages up into neat little compartments and face them one by one. C. S. Lewis, facing his grief over the loss of his wife, wrote *A Grief Observed*. In it, he shows how these stages merge and overlap:

> Tonight, all the hells of young grief have opened again, the mad words, the bitter resentment, the fluttering in the stomach, the nightmare unreality, the wallowed-in tears. For in grief nothing "stays put." One keeps on emerging from a phase, but it always recurs. Round and round. Everything repeats. Am I going in circles, or dare I hope I am on a spiral? But if a spiral, am a going up or down it?[2]

With this in mind, let's look at some of the devils you may meet in the valley of death's dark shadow, remembering all the while there is victory in the valley.

1. A State of Shock

    Our initial response to grief is usually numbness and unbelief. We are in a state of shock and cannot bring ourselves to believe the news is true. This emotion is unhealthy if we continue in it for weeks and absolutely refuse to face the fact of death. But for a few minutes, hours or even days, it is God's gift that helps to soften the blow. We cannot take it all at once, and so the Lord lets the realization of it come gradually. Sooner or later, we face the truth, even though, from time to time, numbness will return momentarily and we will say, "I just can't believe he (she) is gone."

2. An Outburst of Emotion

When the death of a loved one really hits us, we can be caught in the tension of "holding ourselves together" and "letting ourselves go." Like a volcano we want to blow. This feeling is not usually constant, but seems to come and go like the waves on the seashore. Without warning, there wells up within us an uncontrollable urge to express our grief.

My advice to you is, do it! Let yourself go. Cry until you can't cry any more. Beat your pillow until you can't beat your pillow any more. Get your best friend, one who will listen without judging or preaching, and talk to them until you can't talk any more. Go out into the woods or get into the shower and scream until you can't scream any more.

3. The Feeling of Loneliness and Depression

Usually, in our grief, we come to the point that we feel completely isolated and utterly alone. The room may be filled with people, but we are alone. Even those who have lost loved ones, we say, did not love as I loved and did not grieve as I grieve. This feeling of aloneness leads to despair and depression. We feel we have been singled out for a special hurt.

This is a normal reaction to grief. Our love *was* unique. Our grief is unique. We face a fact we cannot change. We face a loss we feel we cannot endure. Depression here is not sin; it is love reaching out for a person we cannot touch. It is sadness, and sadness is not sin, for our Lord was "a man of sorrows, acquainted with grief."

The best hope in this dark hour is that depression will pass. We do not think it will, but it will. We do not think life is worth living, but it is. We do not think we can go on, but we can. If it doesn't, don't be too proud to see a good doctor and to take pills if he prescribes them. They are not permanent. They are like "tire chains" we put on to get us through patchy places of ice on the highway.

Time is the great healer. The sharp, unbearable anguish will pass, but when life deals us this wound, the scar will always remain. There will be throbs and aches during our low moments. But the deep wound itself will heal.

4. Guilt over the Past

One of the worst devils we face in the dark valley, especially if we are Christians, is regret or guilt over the past. We make our departed loved one some kind of supersaint who treated us with nothing but courtesy and kindness. And we make ourselves some kind of supervillain who treated this lovely person with unkindness and indifference.

We begin to wallow in if-onlys. If only I had called the doctor, been there when he died, not been irritable the last time I saw him, loved him more, etc. Regret can rob you of your peace and of your power to go on. There are two things you must do. First, you must accept your loved one's forgiveness. You were not the perfect wife or husband or parent. You did some lousy, nasty things you ought to be ashamed of. But so did the person who died.

Imagine him or her, as he really is, coming back to talk with you. Don't you know they too, now separated from you, would ask your forgiveness for the things they did or failed to do? Wouldn't you forgive them on the spot? Wouldn't you say that, in the light of all the good things you had together, these few bad things are insignificant?

Well, are you better than your loved one? Will you forgive them, but live as though they haven't forgiven you? I do not know if our loved ones in heaven know what is happening to us on earth. But I know we would hurt them and grieve them if we ruin our lives with regrets, feeling that they have not forgiven us or refusing to forgive ourselves. If we persist in guilt, we actually insult our loved one by refusing to accept their forgiveness.

A second thing you might do is confess all your sins against them to the Lord and to them. In addition, tell the Lord and them that you forgive them for all they did to you.

I don't believe in talking to the dead, but I do believe in talking to the Lord, who is in the presence of our dead, who are alive with Him. My mother and I were so much alike that we brought out the worst in each other and found it hard to get along. We said and did many unkind things to each other.

After she went into a coma and died, my regret was almost unbearable. In the grip of great guilt, I knew I was headed for the same depression that helped take her life. I went to her coffin and stayed about an hour. I talked with the Lord and with her. With tears of regret and repentance, I confessed my wrongs and asked for and accepted her forgiveness and the Lord's.

I even talked about the things she had done to me and gave her my forgiveness. That was one of the highest and most beautiful hours of my life. I still have moments of regret. My eyes still swell up with tears when I think of my unkind words and deeds. But I can hear my mother say, "Bobby, I understand. I love you. There is nothing to forgive. I was as lousy a parent as you were a son. The best thing you can do for me is to go on with your life and be a good and a happy person. The worst thing would be for you to ruin your life and happiness because of me."

5. Anger and Bitterness

The most frightening emotion in the valley of grief is anger or bitterness. We find ourselves angry at the doctors or nurses or friends and relatives because they didn't "do more." We are even angry at friends who "say the wrong things" when they try to help.

We even find ourselves angry at God. This is one emotion we are afraid to admit. We say with Job exactly what we are "supposed" to say, "The Lord gave, and the Lord has taken away; blessed be the name of the Lord" (Job. 1:21). This sounded good, but it didn't reflect Job's true, inner feeling. He was acting like he was "supposed" to.

This was not conscious dishonesty. Job felt this way at the moment because he was programmed to. But deep within his soul were some stormy misgivings about the ways of the Almighty. He could quote truths like Romans 8:28 for a while. He could say things like "God never makes a mistake" for a while.

But sooner or later, Job and many of us have to get in touch with deeper, more frightful emotions. We must come face-to-face with the fact of our bitterness and our doubts toward God.

Job did just this. He made some startling statements when the floods of bitterness broke. He cursed the day of his birth (3:1–3); told God to leave him alone (7:16); and cried, "Why use me for your target practice?" (7:20).

Elisabeth Kubler-Ross described her experience with a mother whose small child died:

> She looked very numb, so I said to her, "You look as though you need to scream." And she said, "Do you have a screaming room in the hospital?" She was serious. I said, "No, but we have a chapel," which was a silly answer because she immediately replied, "I need just the opposite. I need to

scream and rage and curse. I've just been sitting in the parking lot and cursing and screaming at God. 'God, why do you let this happen to me?'" And I said, "Do it here. It's better to do it with somebody than out in a parking lot all alone."[3]

I have no neat and tidy answer as to whether such anger and doubt is sinful. I suppose that it is. But I feel it is far more sinful, and I know it is far more harmful to have such feelings and deny them. It is sinful to have doubts and not work through them. It is sinful to have questions of the Father and be afraid to ask them. It is sinful to squelch anger and doubt by quoting a verse or saying, "God never makes a mistake," when you believe He has. No less a Bible-believing conservative than Vance Havner said of the death of his wife:

> Whoever thinks he has the ways of God conveniently tabulated, analyzed and correlated with convenient, glib answers to ease every question from aching hearts has not been far in this maze of mystery we call life and death.[4]

Child of God, it is right to question God if you have questions. Even Jesus and the psalmist asked, "My God! My God! Why hast thou forsaken me?" (Ps. 22:1; Matt. 27:46). The poet said, "Unexamined faith is not worth having." Another said, "There is more faith, believe me, in honest doubt, than in half the creeds."

You should have enough faith in God to be honest with Him and to trust Him to lead you to doubt your doubts and serve Him even if your questions remain unanswered. You may never know why this has happened to you. But if you will honestly and courageously work through your doubt and anger, you will know who is with you. The day will surely come when you will cry out:

> I will not doubt, though all my ships at sea
> Come drifting home, with broken masts and sails;
> I shall believe the Hand which never fails,
> For seeming evil worketh good for me;
> And though I weep because these sails are battered
> Still will I cry, while my best hopes lie shattered,
> "I trust in Thee!"[5]

6. Guilt over the Future

Oddly enough, when we begin to pull ourselves together and life begins to take on meaning, we often feel guilty for returning to hope and happiness. We feel we owe it to our loved one to prove our love by being miserable. Hope begins to break through, but we resist returning.

Here again, we should put ourselves in our loved one's place. The last thing we would want them to do would be to prove their love by their unhappiness. That kind of love is sick. What we would want them to do is built upon what we built and go on to further levels of purposeful and joyful living. We don't want them to pay us back for our love; we want them to pass it on.

III. You Must Face the Future of Grief

The most important word in our text is *through*. The valley has an end. The pain will never completely go away, but it will become bearable and the day will come when you will laugh again without feeling guilty. Life will never be the same, but it can be good.

The Bible's first reference to tears is in Genesis 23:2. When Sarah, Abraham's beloved wife, died, he "went in to mourn for Sarah and to weep for her." He walked through the valley of grief. Then we read, "Then Abraham rose from before his dead and spoke to the sons of Heth" (Gen. 23:3). Here Abraham did two things. He wept over his wife—this is grief. Then he went on with his life—this is healthy recovery.

You may find it hard to believe, but if you commit your grief to God, if you seek His will and search His word, if you allow Him to use it to make you more like Jesus, you can walk out of this valley a better and wiser person. An old Negro preacher put it well. He said, "In the valley you find the 'Lily of the Valley.'" C. S. Lewis said, "God whispers to us in our pleasures, speaks in our conscience, but shouts in our pains."[6]

Like all good things and all character-building processes, this is hard work. "It is a long, slow painful, but worthwhile process," Arthur Freese says in *Help for Your Grief*:

> Grief work is just what it says, the task of mourning. And it is work—hard, long, painful, slow, repetitive, suffering through the same struggle over and over. It is a matter of rethinking and re-feeling, reworking the same long-past fields, the same old emotional material, over and over—breaking through the denial and disbelief that the past and the deceased are both dead.... Out of this a whole new mourner emerges with new attitudes, new concepts, new values, new appreciation of life itself; and if these are better than the old, then there has been growth and change and all the suffering has been worthwhile, then grief has been good.[7]

L. D. Johnson, chaplain of Furman University, lost his daughter Carole in a tragic accident that took her life when she was twenty-three years old. In a beautiful book *The Morning after Death*, which dealt with this, he talked about the beneficial effects of his grief. He talked about how his trip through the valley of grief has made him a better person.

He said it helped him appreciate life both for himself and for his other loved ones. Knowing how soon and how suddenly we, or one we love, can be taken away, grief can teach us to treasure little moments and events in our relationships.

Most of all, he says, we can become ministers to others who grieve. He says, "The healthy-minded griever who has returned from the ranks of the grief-stricken can be a valuable ally to fallen comrades. Not only is he living proof that one can survive the most terrible assaults, but also, he may be a veteran with a kit of very useful survival tools."[8]

God put it this way in 2 Corinthians 1:3–4, "Let us give thanks to…the God from whom all help comes! He helps us in all our troubles, so that we are able to help others…using the same help that we ourselves have received from God" (TEV). In the valley of grief, when we are tempted to give in and give up and give out and quit, our prayer should be:

> O strengthen me, that, while I stand
> Firm on the rock and strong in Thee,
> I may stretch out a loving hand
> To wrestlers with the troubled sea.

NOTES

[1] Gary Collins, *Christian Counseling: A Comprehensive Guide* (Waco, Texas: Word Publishing Company, 1980), 416.
[2] C. S. Lewis, *A Grief Observed* (New York: Bantam Books, 1961), 66, 67.
[3] Elizabeth Kubler-Ross, "What Is It Like to Be Dying?" *American Journal of Nursing* 71, No. 1 (January 1971): 58.
[4] Vance Havner, *Though I Walk Through the Valley* (Old Tappan, NJ: Revell, 1974), 67.
[5] Ella Wheeler Wilcox, *Faith* (Hammond, Indiana: Rand McNally & Company).
[6] C. S. Lewis, *The Problem of Pain* (The Centenary Press, 1940).
[7] Arthur Freese, *Help For Your Grief* (New York: Schocken Books, 1977), 48.
[8] L. D. Johnson, *The Morning after Death* (Broadman Press, 1978).

CHAPTER 2

The Defeat of Death

> Death has been swallowed up in victory. Where, O death, is your victory? Where, O death, is your sting? (1 Cor. 15:54–55)

To find victory in the valley of grief, we need to take a long, hard, and honest look at death. This is something we seldom do. When it is thrust upon us, we tend to see only that which is ugly and horrible and painful. In our better moments, we see it as God sees it, as something beautiful and precious (Ps. 116:15), but then we return to the ugly side of it. This tension between death as ugly and beautiful is something we live with for a while. Victory comes when we are able to see death as God sees it.

Bereavement forces this tension upon us. Even when death sets our dear one free from pain, it is hard to welcome it as a friend. We call death a sweet chariot in our songs, and preachers speak of it as a blessing in disguise. And for those who suffer, death may be welcomed in this way; but for those of us left behind, we see it as an ugly, brutal, heartless thief.

Death may deliver us from pain, but wasn't this pain itself the first touch of death's cold hand? Wasn't the prelude part of the whole drama? How can we call "friend" the God who struck our loved one down in the prime of life, put him in the hospital, and finally took his life? We can soften the blow and help remove the sting by remembering first the following:

The Defeat of Death

I. Death Is Natural and Universal

The Bible teaches what we already know, that death comes to all of us. It is a natural part of life. The Bible says there is "a time to be born and a time to die" (Eccles. 3:2). It says it "is appointed unto men once to die" (Heb. 9:27).

With the exception of Enoch (Gen. 5:24) and Elijah (2 Kings 2:11), every single member of the human race has had to go through death. Thus, you have not been singled out. God is not using you for target practice (Job. 6:4, 7:20 TEV). The grim statistics are simple: one out of every one of us dies.

A man lost his wife and kept saying, "Why me? Why me?" One day the thought hit him, *Why not me?* He slowly saw the truth that he was no different and no better or worse than untold millions who had walked this road. He knew he had not been singled out. His bitterness slowly departed, peace settled in, and he went on with his life.

The first step in facing and defeating death is to see it realistically as something natural and universal. It is part of the price we pay for life. Your loved one has simply made a journey we must all make.

II. Death Is the Result of the Fall

The word *natural* can be misleading. By death being natural, we mean it is part of the nature of things as they are. There is something divine in our souls however that recoils from death. To us, it is unnatural. It is an intruder. It is part of God's judgment on sin (Gen. 2:17). It is dreadfully pictured as a pale horse (Rev. 6:8) and is called our enemy (1 Cor. 15:26).

This is because the death of human beings is not part of the nature of things as they are intended to be. Theologians argue the point, but the Bible seems to teach that Adam and Eve were not created to die. God told them, "When you eat of it (the forbidden tree) you will surely die" (Gen. 2:17).

When they disobeyed God, the process of death began to work in their bodies and part of God's pronounced judgment was, "You will eat your food until you return to the ground, since from it you were taken; for dust you are and to dust you will return" (Gen. 3:19). Paul said, "Therefore, just as sin entered the world through one man, and death through sin, and in this way death came to all men" (Rom. 5:12).

A. H. Strong says the translation of Enoch and Elijah and the Christians who are "alive and caught up" at the Second Coming of Christ "seems intended to teach us that death is not a necessary law and to show what would have happened to Adam if he had been obedient."

This explains our confusion and our tension. We are torn in two directions. Death is both natural and unnatural. As children of mankind, it is a law of life. As children of God, it is an intruder that does not belong.

One thing must be made clear. While death is part of God's punishment upon the human race, it is not a punishment for the Christian. It is an enemy we face (1 Cor. 15:26), but our struggle with him is intended to make us stronger and better. The Christian may be disciplined, but he is never punished. A. H. Strong says, "When death becomes the property of the believer, it receives a new name, and is called sleep."

III. Death Is a Blessed Experience

We move now from the general to the particular. Let us take the Word of God, go to the moment of death your loved one experienced, and see what death really was.

A martyr was being led through the streets to the gallows. All around him, people stood weeping and moaning. He stopped, looked them in the face and said, "This is my coronation day. Isn't there anyone here who will praise God with me?"

If our loved ones could speak to us across the Great Divide, I believe they would say, "I know you are sad. I know the loneliness is hard to bear. But when you think of me and who I am now and where I am now, I want you to be happy for me and to praise God."

How can this be? How could Paul "desire to depart and be with Christ" (Phil. 1:23)? How can God see the death of His saints as precious (Ps. 116:15)? From an earthly point of view, as we think about such things as caskets and graves and empty places at the table, something dreadful has happened to those we love.

From a heavenly, biblical point of view, however, something wonderful has happened. From God's point of view and our loved ones' point of view, what exactly is death?

1. Death Is a Peaceful Experience (1 Cor. 15:55).

    Because death is not God's punishment of a Christian, it is not something we have to fear. Thus, Jesus could leave Gethsemane for Calvary, saying, "Arise! Let us go!" (Matt. 26:46). Thus, Paul could say, "O, death, where is your sting?" (1 Cor. 15:55).

    Here we have a problem. Most of us, in our better moments, must admit that we do fear death. We are like the old sharecropper. Walking out of the field one evening with a heavy cotton sack on his back, he said, "Oh God, I wish I was dead!" Suddenly, there before him stood the angel of death.

    "What is it you want?" the angel said.

    "Two things," the man replied. "This sack on my back and my feet on this field."

    He wasn't as unafraid of or as ready for death as he thought he was.

    Is it wrong for us to have a fear of death or to desire life over death? I do not think so. While God doesn't want us to have a morbid dread of dying, I believe He expects us to have a healthy apprehension about dying and a desire to keep on living. Before Moses died, he told his people, "I have set before you life and death, blessing and cursing; therefore, *choose life*" (Deut. 30:19).

    A good healthy respect for (or fear of) death is what has helped build hospitals, educate doctors, prevent suicides, and made philosophers out of most of us. Lofton Hudson is right, "If we were not shocked at death, life would be in jeopardy.... To the extent that we are committed to life, we foster good health habits, (and) search for peaceful means of settling disputes."[1]

Why then did Paul go beyond being unafraid to actually desiring to die? It was because he believed himself to be at the point of death and God gave him dying grace. Someone asked D. L. Moody if he had the grace to die. Moody said he did not have it and he did not want it. He wanted the grace of God to enable him to live in Chicago and preach the Gospel.

Moody then said, "When my time comes to die, then I shall want dying grace, and I believe I shall have it." Just before he died, Moody said, "I see earth receding. Heaven is opening. God is calling." He had dying grace when death came. It is when we "walk" through the valley of the shadow of death that we are not afraid (Ps. 23).

Paul challenged the enemy and said, "Where, O death, is your victory? Where, O death, is your sting? The sting of death is sin" (1 Cor. 15:55, 56). Christ does not save us from death but from the dread and the fear of death. It is not our punishment; it is our purifier, making us more like our Lord. It is our pathway to perfection and, most of all, to the presence of our Lord, who went through death before us and waits for us on the other side (John 14:3).

It should be a great source of encouragement and comfort for you to know that your loved one, in Christ, died unafraid. God's will did not put them where God's grace could not sustain them. This is especially true if you were not with them when they died. In my twenty-two years as a pastor, I have walked in the valley with many a dying child of God. Not a single, solitary one was gripped by fear.

The famous physician Sir William Osler had his nurse record the deaths of five hundred persons. Some feared death before, but only a few showed fear when death actually arrived. Invariably, dying was peaceful and painless.

Dr. Charles Allen went to visit one of his older members in the hospital. Time had taken its toll upon her body but not upon her spirit. Death was a great possibility in her case, and when the subject came up, she said, "Dr. Allen, the Father's house is mighty attractive to me now." Looking at death, for the Christian, we see it as something peaceful. In addition, we see that…

2. Death Is Falling Asleep (Acts 7:60).

The Bible describes death as a "falling asleep." Describing the agonizing death of Stephen, the scripture says, "He fell asleep" (Acts 7:60).

The Greek word for falling asleep is *koimao* and for a "sleeping place," it is *koimeterion*. From this, we get our word *cemetery*. The idea of death as sleep in scripture refers primarily to our bodies as they lie in the grave and wait for the resurrection. But in the case of Stephen, it referred also to the way he died. Surrounded by enemies and beaten with jagged stones, he fell asleep in Jesus.

Our Lord died much the same way. His final word from the cross was, "Father, into thy hands, I commend my spirit" (Luke 23:46). This was a quotation from Psalm 31, but more than this, it was part of a childhood prayer that every devout Jewish mother taught her child to pray at bedtime. Jesus died like a little child going to sleep in his mother's arms.

Peter Marshall preached a sermon called "Go Down, Death." In it, he tells the story of a little boy with an incurable illness. One day the little lad quietly asked his mother, "Mother, what is it like to die? Does it hurt?" Making some excuse, she fled into the hall and tried to brush back the tears. Knowing she had to answer him, she regained her courage and went back in.

She said, "Kenneth, do you remember how you would play so hard that after supper you would fall asleep on Mama and Daddy's bed with your clothes on? The next morning you woke up in your own bed. Daddy had come and with his strong arms had carried you to your room.

Kenneth, death is like that. We go to sleep down here. Jesus comes and gets us, and we wake up in another room up above." The little boy never asked another question about death, and a few days later, he just went to sleep and went to be with Jesus.

3. Death Is the Departure to True Life (2 Tim. 4:6).

Finally, we are not to fear death or give in to bitterness over the death of someone we love because death is the doorway to true life. It is a valley we pass "through."

Paul called it a departure. He said, "The time of my departure is at hand" (2 Tim. 4:6). He also called it a change of houses. He said, "Now we know that if the earthly tent we live in (our body) is destroyed, we have a building from God, an eternal house in heaven, not built by human hands" (1 Cor. 5:1). Jesus said much the same thing: "In my Father's house are many rooms; if it were not so, I would have told you. I am going there to prepare a place for you" (John 14:2).

In our day, many people seem to have passed through death's doorway for a few moments and come back to tell us what is was like. Raymond Moody gives their consistent testimony in his book *Life after Life*. Hundreds of people, from every reach of life, speak of their spirits being separated from their bodies, of passing through a long tunnel, of approaching a bright light, and of being in the presence of immeasurable love.

Now Christians should not base their hopes upon the experiences or the testimony of others. Our hope is based upon the Truth of God's Word. But there is much in all this that squares with the Bible. Let's see exactly what the Bible says about what happened to the one you love. Go to the exact moment of their death. Witness their departure. Look at what happened to them, and you will find peace. In this departure, there is first the following:

The Defeat of Death

1) The Separation of the Spirit from the Body (2 Cor. 5:8)

Death, according to the Bible, is not destruction or annihilation, but separation. The Greek word for death *thanatos* literally means "separation." Death is the separation of our immaterial (spirit) from our material (body).

The Old Testament says, "Then shall the dust return to the earth as it was; and the spirit shall return unto God who gave it" (Eccles. 12:7). Paul said that to be "absent from the body" was to be "present with the Lord" (2 Cor. 5:8). Death, for him, meant to "depart and be with Christ" (Phil. 1:23). When Jesus died on the cross, His body went limp and lifeless, and was fit only for burial and subsequent decay. But how did He die? What was death for Him? He said in dying, "Father, into thy hands I commit my spirit" (Luke 23:46).

All of this means that the one we loved and lost was never put in a coffin and never put in the ground. There is not one single solitary person in any graveyard, anywhere. Jesus Christ was never in the grave. They put His body there, but the Bible says, "He was put to death in the body, but made alive in the spirit, in which he also went and made proclamation to the spirits now in prison" (1 Pet. 3:18, 19). The day Jesus died (Friday), they took his body down and buried it, but Jesus told the thief that day (Friday), "Today (Friday) you will be with me in Paradise" (Luke 23:43).

It is right to grieve over our loved one's body and pay respect to it (Luke 24:1). But it is wrong to be morbid and live at the cemetery. This can degenerate into grieving "as those who have no hope" (1 Thess. 4:13). Edwin Markham said it well:

> Let us not think of our departed dead
> As caught and cumbered in their graves of earth;
> But think of death as of another birth,
> As a new freedom for the wings outspread,
> A new adventure waiting on ahead,

As a new joy of more ethereal mirth,
As a new world with friends of nobler worth,
Where all may taste a more immortal bread.
So, comrades, if you pass my grave sometime,
Pause long enough to breathe this little rhyme:
"Here now the dust of Edwin Markham lies,
But lo, he is not here: he is afar
On life's great errands under mightier skies,
And pressing on toward some melodious star."[2]

2) The Meeting with Jesus (John 14:3)

In this departure there is, second, the meeting with Jesus. When our spirit leaves our body and starts through the doorway of eternity, it meets the Lord. In John 14:3, Jesus told His disciples, "And if I go and prepare a place for you, I will come again and receive you to Myself; that where I am you maybe also." This particular verse does not refer to the Second Coming at the end of the world. It refers to the coming of Jesus Christ to meet us in the hour of death. Arthur Pink says, "The Lord will not send for us, but come in person to conduct us to the Father's House. How precious we must be to Him."

This tells us something beautiful about death. The one you love did not die alone. This is one of our great fears. It is why the American Indians buried their dead with familiar items such as beads and bow and arrows. It is why the Pharaohs were buried with their wives. It is why we so desperately want to be with people when they die. We want them to know they are not alone.

The sad truth is, from a human point of view, we all die alone. The room can be filled with familiar faces and our hands can be held by those we love. And yet we still slip into the next world all by ourselves. We leave those we love behind.

But the moment we turn from the faces and hands of those we know and love, we turn to the face and hands

The Defeat of Death

of the Lord Jesus Christ. As David said, "Yea, tho I walk through the valley of the shadow of death, I will fear no evil, for Thou art with me" (Ps. 23). The grand old hymn put it well:

> I won't have to cross Jordan alone
> Jesus died for my sins to atone
> In the darkness I see He'll be waiting for me.
> I won't have to cross Jordan alone.

In reality, you have not given the one you love to the ugly Grim Reaper we call death. You have given them to the beautiful Savior we call Jesus.

Dr. Roy McClain tells of the parents who heard the awful verdict, "Your little girl is incurably ill." After days of agony, they submitted and accepted it as the will of God. Then came the awful question: "Should we tell her? She is only nine years old. Should we prepare her? How do you tell a nine-year-old little girl she is going to die?"

Mustering the necessary courage, they sat down with her, and in the quiet of her room, the father said, "Darling, I have something hard to tell you. The doctors tell us you have a disease they cannot cure. We have asked God to heal you, but it seems that His will is to take you to heaven to be with Him. Pretty soon He will send a long train to get you and take you to the beautiful city where He and His angels live."

Quick as a flash, the frightened little girl said, "Daddy, will Jesus be at the station to meet me?"

"You bet He will!" the father quickly replied. "And what's more, Mother and Daddy will be on the very next train to join you."

3) The Entrance into Heaven (Heb. 12:22, 23)

Finally, when our spirit leaves its body and meets the Lord, it enters into heaven. (See the next chapter that discusses this "intermediate state" and the final one, which discusses the joys of heaven.) What Jesus said to the dying thief on the cross, He can say to each of us, "Today, you will be with me in Paradise" (Luke 23:43). He takes us to the "heavenly Jerusalem," to the dwelling place of "the spirits of righteous men made perfect" (Heb. 12:22, 23), to our room in the Father's house (John 14:2).

More will be said about the glories of heaven in our final chapter. But for right now, think of the truth that you have lost the one you love not to the grave, not to the dim unknown, and not even to "the great Someone in the great somewhere," but to Jesus Christ in heaven. Go back to the moment of their death. See their beautiful spirit leave their body. See them as they see Jesus and take His hand. And see them arrive in heaven, taking their first glimpse of glory!

> Think of stepping on shore and finding it Heaven!
> Of taking hold of a hand and finding it God's!
> Of breathing new air and finding it celestial air!
> Of feeling invigorated and finding it immortality!
> Of passing from storm and stress to a perfect calm!
> Of waking and finding it Home![3]

4) The Teacher of Those Left Behind (Rom. 8:28)

We have gone bravely to the moment of your loved one's death. We have looked the Grim Reaper in the face. And because of God's dying grace, because the spirit survived death, because of the meeting with Jesus, and because of the joys in heaven right now, we can say, "O death! Where is thy sting?"

Now, as you walk away and try to resume your life, I want you to think of your loved one's death and how many good and useful things it can teach you. The whole experience can make you bitter or it can make you better. It's up to you. God can make even this work together for your good (Rom. 8:28).

The Defeat of Death

After John and Frances Gunther lost their seventeen-year-old son to cancer, Frances wrote, "Death always brings one suddenly face to face with life. Nothing, not even the birth of one's child, brings one so close to life as death."

Dear friend, you have paid the price. Buy something with it. Let your loved one be a blessing to you even in their death. If you come out of this experience with new attitudes, new values, new appreciations of life and deeper faith in the reality of the Christian faith and the hereafter, then your suffering will be worthwhile, and new meaning will be added to your loved one's death.

NOTES

[1] R. Lofton Hudson, *Persons in Crisis* (Nashville, Tennessee: Broadman Press, 1969), 117.
[2] Quoted in *The Funeral Encyclopedia: A Sourcebook* (Grand Rapids, Michigan: Baker Book House, 1953).
[3] L. E. Singer, "Finally Home" (Singspiration, 1971).

CHAPTER 3

Joy Right Now in the New Jerusalem

> But you have come to Mount Zion, to the heavenly Jerusalem, the city of the living God. You have come to thousands upon thousands of angels in joyful assembly, to the church of the firstborn, whose names are written in heaven. You have come to God, the judge of all men, TO THE SPIRITS OF RIGHTEOUS MEN MADE PERFECT, to Jesus the mediator of a new covenant. (Heb. 12:22–24)

The Bible says much about our hope of heaven. We look forward to that day when we shall be with each other and with our Lord in glory. But what about right now? We need the added comfort of having some knowledge about the location and activities of our departed loved ones right now. In theological terms, this present time period between death and the future resurrection and eternal age is called the intermediate state.

The Bible does not tell us a great deal about the present state of those who have died. It gives us only a few brief glimpses. Since it is describing a world far different from ours, it uses symbols and pictures and analogies that can give us only a portion of the truth. Because of this, there is confusion and disagreement among students of the Bible. I hope the brief remarks here will give you comfort, for I believe I can show you that there is joy right now for your departed loved one in the heavenly Jerusalem.

For any kind of an answer about the dead, we must turn to the Word of God. Man's knowledge ends at the graveyard. The sum total of his wisdom about the dead is "ashes to ashes, dust to dust." But the God who wrote the Bible, the God who became a human being, the God who tasted death and came back and forth between the beyond and here, the God-man Jesus can tell us about it. He is God over "there," wherever "there" is, just as He is God over here.

The same One who created what we know over here, created whatever there is over there. And so we turn to His Word and ask, "Where are our beloved dead right now?"

I. They Are in Heaven (Heb. 12:22–24)

God's first response is, "They are in heaven." They are in the heavenly Jerusalem (Heb. 12:22–24), which both Jesus (Luke 23:43) and the book of Revelation (Rev. 2:7, 22:2) called Paradise. They are in the garden spot of the universe.

We are afraid to believe this because some Bible students stick Paradise off in some compartment of the land of the dead (what the Old Testament calls Sheol). But when you compare scripture with scripture, you see that departed Christians are with their Lord, with their fellow believers, with God, and with the angels in heaven. They experience and express the joys of the New Jerusalem. This is the express teaching of our text (Heb. 12:22–24). Now let's examine this point by point.

1. Their Heaven Is Pictured as the Heavenly Jerusalem.

    In Revelation 21, we have a picture of the future state, after the return of Christ, in the era of the "new heaven and the new earth" (Rev. 21:1). And down to this earth descends "the holy city, the new Jerusalem" (21:2). Like the ancient Jews, we have a city. It is a city that we will one day possess with all the people of God when this age of sin and sorrow are past (Rev. 21:4, 22:14–15). But the book of Hebrews teaches we have that city right now. Every time we look to God in worship and prayer, we are like Daniel who prayed with his face turned toward Jerusalem (Dan. 6:10). This is why the book of Hebrews says, "You *have come* to Mount Zion, to the heavenly Jerusalem, the city of the living God" (12:22).

And when we die, we go to that city. There we find, "the spirits of righteous men made perfect" (Heb. 12:23). You ask me where it is! I do not know. I don't know if it is "out there," or "up there" or "down there." But I do know it is somewhere. You won't find it on any map of the universe. You won't go there in any spacecraft built by NASA. But it is as real a city as New York; London; or Anderson, South Carolina. And it is the home address of our beloved Christian dead. Our Lord said, "I go and prepare a *place* for you" (John 14:2). Our loved ones are not with "Someone in the great somewhere," they are with the Lord God in the heavenly Jerusalem.

2. Their Heaven Is Pictured as Paradise (Luke 23:43; 2 Cor. 12:2–4; Rev. 2:7, 22:2).

God's word for the heavenly Jerusalem is *Paradise*. When the thief on the cross put his faith in Christ, Jesus said to him, "This day you will be with Me in Paradise" (Luke 23:43). When Jesus died He went through the gates of glory (Ps. 24:7–10). His spirit went to the Father (Luke 23:46). His word for this destination was Paradise.

When the apostle Paul had what could well have been an after-death experience, in one of those episodes when he was thought dead (Acts 14:19), he said, "Whether it was in the body or out of the body I do not know…this man (himself) was caught up to Paradise" (2 Cor. 12:2–3).

Earlier he had described this as being caught up into "the third heaven" (2 Cor. 12:2). For the Jews, there were three heavens. The first was atmospheric where the birds fly. The second was the stellar heaven where the stars dwell. The third heaven was the highest heaven, the heaven beyond our physical universe where God lives. And Paul's name for this heaven is Paradise.

In the book of Revelation, God tells the church at Ephesus that they may "eat of the tree of life, which is in the Paradise of God" (Rev. 2:7). Later, He tells us (Rev. 22:2) that the tree of life is on each side of the river that flows from the throne of God in the heavenly Jerusalem. This then is Paradise.

Our loved ones are in heaven, the garden spot of God's universe. Certainly, they are not reaping the full blessings that are yet to come. For one thing, heaven is incomplete because you and I and others are still on the way. For another thing, they have more reward to receive. The influence of their lives is still going on. The Bible says, "Blessed are the dead who die in the Lord…their deeds will follow them" (Rev. 14:13). They will have more joy as they see us come to be with them. They will receive, if they have been faithful, more rewards at the judgment day. As full as they are, they have more blessings to come. We admit this. But we should also not hesitate to confess, "Our departed dead are in heaven, in the city of the living God, living with the Lord and singing praises with the angels."

II. They Are with God (Heb. 12:23)

Our text tells us that to be in the heavenly Jerusalem is to be with God (12:23). This statement seems almost absurd because God is everywhere. This is true. But it is also true that God, who cannot be seen (Jn. 1:18), has chosen to manifest His glory before the eyes of men. It was His Shekinah glory that appeared to Israel as a burning pillar of fire (Exod. 13:21–22). When Stephen died and Jesus stood up in the heavenly Jerusalem, the scripture says, "But Stephen, full of the Holy Spirit, looked up to heaven and saw the *glory of God* and Jesus standing at the right hand of God" (Acts 7:55). This glory is the light of heaven (Rev. 22:5), and our loved ones live in the glow of the light of the glory of God right now.

III. They Are with Jesus (Luke 23:43)

Unable to see the invisible God and able only to live close to His glory, they are able to see, touch, talk with, and fellowship with Jesus. He is God made manifest in human form (John 1:14). In Him, they behold the glory in human terms (John 1:14). He is the "image of the invisible God" (Col. 1:15). He is the outshining of the glory of God (Heb. 1:3).

It should be a source of unspeakable joy to know that our loved ones are with the Lord. Jesus told the dying thief, "Today, you will be *with me* in Paradise" (Luke 23:43). Paul said he wanted "to be absent from the body and at home with the Lord" (2 Cor. 5:8).

My favorite verse in this connection is John 14:3, where our Lord says, "If I go and prepare a place for you, I will come again and will receive you unto myself, that where I am, there you may be also." I do not believe that this verse deals with the Second Coming but with the hour of death when Jesus comes to claim His own. When a Christian closes his eyes in death, the first sight he sees on the other side is the face of Jesus Christ. Our first glimpse of glory is the glorious face of our Redeemer. I believe the humblest believer at his death shall have the same vision that Stephen had. "Look!" he said. "I see heaven opened and the Son of Man standing at the right hand of God" (Acts 7:56). For this reason we can sing,

> When I come to the river at closing of day
> When the last winds of sorrow have blown
> There'll be Somebody waiting to show me the way
> I won't have to cross Jordan alone.

IV. They Are with Fellow Christians (Heb. 12:22–24)

The "spirits of just men made perfect" live in a city. This speaks of joyful community and fellowship. Heaven is not a crowd. It is a family. God calls us all by name. We know each other by name. On the Mount of Transfiguration, Peter and John recognized Moses and Elijah and called them by name.

Think of all the good and godly people you have known who have died. What a noble band! What a group to be with! And that is where your loved one is right now.

> It is not death to die
> To leave this weary road
> And, midst the brotherhood on high
> To be at home with God.[1]

And best of all, dear friend, they have not completely left you. You hold them in your heart, and they hold you in theirs. Sweet memories pass both ways between heaven and earth and keep love alive. And they are waiting for you. Say this:

> I cannot think of them as dead
> Who walk with me no more
> Along the path of life I tread
> They have but gone before.
> The Father's house is mansioned fair
> Beyond my vision dim
> All souls are His, and here or there
> Are living unto Him.
> And still their silent ministry
> Within my heart hath place
> As when on earth they walked with me
> And met me face to face.[2]

V. They Are Conscious (Rev. 6:9–10)

Because the Bible often speaks of death as "sleep" (Deut. 31:16), many Protestants believe our departed dead right now are asleep. This is the doctrine known as soul sleep. Examining scripture with scripture, it seems that the term *sleep* applies primarily to the body or to the peaceful manner in which one dies (Acts 7:60), but that the soul after death is awake and conscious and active. In Revelation 6:9–10, the Christian dead ask questions. In Revelation 7:15, they are said to be serving God day and night.

A beautiful passage in Revelation says they "rest from their labors" (Rev. 14:13. See also 6:11). The Greek word can mean "refreshed" or "rested." In the Greek, it was used of the sailor who had come through the trouble seas to find rest in port. This tells me our loved ones in heaven are not tired and weary and worn.

Spurgeon said that when he got to heaven, he wanted to sleep for a thousand years. I believe that when he got there, he felt like he had. Our loved ones are alive and refreshed and full of new strength and are ready to serve a million years without a trace of weariness.

VI. Are They Bodiless? (2 Cor. 5:1–6)

An unanswerable question is whether or not our departed dead have a recognizable form or body at this time. Protestant theology has leaned toward the fact that they do not. In fact, many works of theology call this intermediate state the disembodied state.

Certainly they do not have their final resurrection body with which they will inhabit eternity when this age is over. That body will be fashioned out of the particles that are now resting in the earth. Paul said, "The body that is sown is perishable, it is raised imperishable; it is sown in dishonor, it is raised in glory; it is sown in weakness, it is raised in power; it is sown a natural body, it is raised a spiritual body" (1 Cor. 15:42–44). All of this takes place at the Second Coming of Jesus Christ "at the last trumpet" (1 Cor. 15:52).

But what about right now? Must we try and visualize our loved ones as invisible spirits with no form or shape? The scripture gives us several hints that we do not. Our departed dead seem to have some visible form, some intermediate kind of spiritual body.

In 2 Corinthians 5:1–6, Paul is talking about death and describes it as leaving this "earthly tent." Then he says of the heavenly body: "We have a building from God, an eternal house in heaven, not built by human hands. Meanwhile we groan, longing to be clothed with our heavenly dwelling, because when we are clothed, we will not be found naked" (2 Cor. 5:1–3).

Now Paul could be talking about the final resurrection body. But two things stand out here to me. First, he says we "have" a body in heaven, and he uses the present tense. We have it now. It is waiting for us. Second, he draws back and seems repelled by the idea of being "naked" or not having a body to clothe his spirit.

In the book of Revelation, we are told of the souls of the martyrs under the altar of God in heaven. The Bible says, "Then each of them was given a white robe" (Rev. 6:11). This white robe could be symbolic of salvation (7:14) but could also point to their heavenly clothing that covers their heavenly bodies in this interim period. When Moses and Elijah appeared to Jesus on the Mount of Transfiguration, they had identifiable, tangible, real bodies.

My advice to you is to not get all tangled up in this theological debate. Visualize your loved one in glory as he or she appeared to you on earth. Subtract sorrow and sin and weariness and worry and burden and see them joyful and thankful and useful and beautiful as they praise God (Rev. 7:9–10) and serve God (Rev. 7:15) and wait for you and me (Rev. 6:11). Though their bodies lie in the grave and wait for the resurrection morning, I believe with all my heart that when your spirit leaves your body in death and you pass to the other side, you will be able to see and embrace and talk with your loved ones and they with you. The "how" of this, I simply leave with God.

VII. Are They Aware of Earth? (Heb. 12:1)

Another difficult question is whether or not our loved ones are aware of what is happening to us on earth right now. In Revelation 6:10, they seem to remember the earthly struggles and have pity for us as they cry out, "How long, Sovereign Lord, holy and true, until you judge the inhabitants of earth and avenge our blood?"

The classic passage is Hebrews 12:1. In chapter 11, God tells us about the heroes of the Old Testament. In chapter 12, he challenges us to follow in their footsteps and "run with perseverance the race that is set before us" (12:1). In between, in Hebrews 12:1, he says, "Therefore, since we are surrounded by such a great cloud of witnesses," let us run the race well.

The picture is taken from the athletic games of Greece. And some take the meaning literally. In the heavenly grandstand, the Christians in heaven are watching us and praying for us and cheering us on. The great Presbyterian preacher Clarence Macartney said, "I have little doubt that they observe our life here in this world."

Others feel that "witness" does not mean they are "spectators" who witness or watch what we do. They bore their witness in the earth, and in heaven, they are our examples.

I tend to believe the last view. God definitely forbids our trying to communicate with the dead (Deut. 18). I cannot see them sitting in heaven with the omniscience of God knowing and seeing every little thing we do. I do see them, however, remembering us and concerned for us (Rev. 6:10). And I see Jesus, with them, telling them whatever they need to know about us.

I love to play in our church golf tournaments. Playing through eighteen holes of golf is, for me, a hard, frustrating but happy experience. But at last, you play the last hole and then sit on the hill in the shade with others who have finished before you. You get a cold drink and a good seat and you watch your fellow golfers, still coming as they hit the ball to the eighteenth hole. You cheer them on and kid them and see them smile and welcome them as they take their seat beside you.

Now all back through that course are your friends still playing golf, even though you can't see them. You know what they are going through. They are having some good moments. They are making long, straight drives; sinking long, difficult putts; getting closer friendships with their playing partners; and stopping for some good, cold drinks of water. But there are some bad things happening too.

There are crooked drives and missed putts. There are blisters and bee stings and aggravations with others on the course.

But these bad memories and realizations of what they are going through don't rob you of your peace about them. For you see, you have made the course. You, with your blisters and bad shots and broken clubs, have made it and enjoyed it; and you know your brothers will too. You can't wait to see them come around the bend and tee off on old "eighteen." You can't wait to welcome them to the "hill" so you can talk about the eighteen holes, good and bad.

Somewhere on the hillsides of glory are our brothers and sisters who have played life's eighteen. They know what we who are still playing are going through. But they know, no matter how bad things get, God will see us through. They know the day will come when we will round the bend and play our last hole. And with joy, they will receive us and welcome us as we take our seat with them on the hillside of glory. I don't know about you, but I can hear them singing as they think about our life and watch us pass from earth to heaven:

> Ten thousand times ten thousand
> In sparkling raiment bright
> The armies of the ransomed saints
> Throng up the steeps of light
> 'Tis finished, all is finished
> Their fight with death and sin
> Fling open wide the golden gates
> And let the victors in.

There is joy right now in the New Jerusalem. And there will be a special and a very personal joy for those we love who are there on that day when we go to be with them. Until then, let us "run with perseverance the race that is set before us."

NOTES

[1] George Washington Bethune, quoted in *The Funeral Encyclopedia: A Sourcebook*, 220.
[2] Frederick L. Hosmer, *Friends Beyond* (New York City: Harper & Row Publishers Incorporated).

CHAPTER 4

The Hope of Heaven

> If only for this life we have hope in Christ, we are to be pitied more than all men. (1 Cor. 15:19)

The ultimate hope of the child of God as he braves the bitter battle of grief is heaven. We need to be made better by grief. We need to look honestly at death. We need to know a little about the joy right now in the heavenly Jerusalem. But after all is said and done, the "light at the end of our tunnel" is heaven. This is not "pie in the sky, by and by" as our critics charge. It is the only thing that makes this "trail of tears" we call life, make any sense. Paul said, "If only for this life we have hope in Christ, we are to be pitied more than all men" (1 Cor. 15:19). The hymn writer said,

> When we all get to heaven
> What a day of rejoicing that will be
> When we all see Jesus,
> We'll sing and shout the victory.

Just as the unborn babe in his mother's womb knows very little about the outside world for which he has been fashioned, so do we know very little about the heaven for which we are being fashioned. God does not tell us much in His Word. There are many interesting but unanswerable questions about our heavenly home. Will there be children in heaven? Or will children who die grow to maturity?

Children ask, "Will my puppy be in heaven?" To these and other questions, we can only answer, "I do not know."

God, however, does tell us what we need to know. Our knowledge is not exhaustive, but it is sufficient. He tells us enough to set our souls rejoicing. He gives us a few "glimpses of glory." Today we shall see what God tells us about what He has in store for us. We will look at our hope of heaven.

I. A Place

First and foremost, heaven is a place. It is called by such names as Paradise (Luke 23:43), glory (Col. 3:4), rest (Heb. 4:9), the kingdom (Matt. 25:34), the Father's house (John 14:2), and the holy city (Rev. 21:2).

When the Bible talks about the "heavens" in verses like Genesis 1:1, it is talking about what we call the universe. God created the atmospheric heaven directly above us. He created the stellar heaven where the stars travel through space.

But above and beyond and far different from these first two heavens is the "third heaven" Paul talked about (2 Cor. 12:2) where God dwells with His people. (See Acts 8:39; Deut. 10:14; Ps. 148:4).

Now this third heaven cannot be seen by any telescope or visited by any spacecraft, but this does not mean it isn't as real a place as London or Paris. I believe it is a real place for several reasons.

1. The Teachings of Scripture

    First is the plain teaching of scripture. Jesus said in John 14:2–3, "I go to prepare a place for you…that you maybe where I am." He talked about people in heaven sitting down to eat with Abraham, Isaac, and Jacob (Matt. 8:11). He promised His disciples at the Last Supper that He would drink the fruit of the vine with them in the Father's kingdom (Matt. 26:29).

2. The Place of Earth in the Final Heaven

I believe heaven is a place, second, because in the end, at the consummation of this age, it includes this universe in which we now live. The Bible tells us that when Jesus comes, He will purge or renovate this universe by fire. Peter says,

> But the day of the Lord will come like a thief. The heavens (universe) will disappear with a loud noise. The elements will be dissolved by fire, and the earth and everything in it will be burned up. (2 Pet. 3:10)

But this is not the final word. Peter goes on, "But in keeping with His promise, we are looking forward to a new heaven and a new earth, the home of righteousness" (2 Pet. 3:13). God will purge this universe of sin and suffering and then give it back to us. And part of this holy, redeemed universe will be the New Jerusalem where are beloved dead are right now (Heb. 12:22–24). John, in Revelation 20, tells us what will happen after the fire falls (Rev. 20:9) and the judgment is over (20:11–15):

> Then I saw a new heaven and a new earth, for the first heaven and the first earth had passed away, and there was no more sea. I saw the Holy City (Of Heb. 12) coming down out of heaven from Go.... And I heard a loud voice from the throne saying, 'Now the dwelling place of God is with man; and he will live with them. They will be his people and He will be their God. He will wipe every tear from their eyes. There will be no more death or mourning, or crying or pain, for the old order of things has passed away. (Rev. 21: 1ff)

When we are talking about heaven, we are talking about a place. It the end, it will include earth. Right now, we enter and live in that city "in the spirit" (2 Cor. 12ff). But one day it will come down to earth.

3. The Resurrection of the Body

Heaven is a place, third, because God is going to give us an identifiable resurrection body. The Bible does not just teach the immortality of the soul, or spirit, or person; it teaches the retrieval, the renewal, and the resurrecting of the body planted in the earth. Paul said,

> We eagerly wait for a Savior from there (heaven), the Lord Jesus Christ, who by the power than enables Him to bring everything under his control; will transform our lowly bodies, so they will be like His glorious body. (Phil. 3:21)

When Jesus comes He will bring with Him the spirits of those who have died and have been living with Him in the heavenly Jerusalem (Heb. 12:22–24; 1 Thess. 4:14). Their bodies will come out of the grave, be changed into resurrection bodies, and will clothe their spirits (John 5:28–29; John 11:24; 1 Cor. 6:14). Paul says of the buried body:

> The body that is sown is perishable, it is raised imperishable; it is sown in dishonor, it is raised in glory; it is sown in weakness, it is raised in power; it is sown a natural body, it is raised a spiritual body. (1 Cor. 15:42–44)

Many questions come to mind. We ask, "How can God reclaim all these particles, some of which have been scattered to the ends of the earth?" The Bible answers,

"Why should any of you consider it incredible that God raises the dead?" (Acts 26:8). We ask what kind of body is it? Paul tells us we are "fools" (1 Cor. 15:35–36) if we think we can know this. He says comparing our present body to our future body is like comparing an acorn to an oak tree (1 Cor. 15:37–38). He says it is not "flesh and blood" (1 Cor. 15:50); it is a "spiritual" body (1 Cor. 15:44).

Let us move from all this speculation to the glorious reality that you will see and touch and know and embrace both the ones you love and the Lord Jesus in heaven. With all that we do not know, we do know this.

It is a very sad thing not to emphasize the resurrection of the body. I am not a graveyard person. I do not believe any of my loved ones are there. But a precious part of them is there. That which I can see and touch and talk with is there. And their precious bodies, changed and cleansed of all imperfections, will rise one day so we can be together. The great evangelist Dwight L. Moody said it well:

> My heaven is a solid heaven. After the resurrection has come, you will have a resurrection foot and something to tread on; a resurrection eye and colors and substances to see with it, a resurrection ear and voices and music to regale it, a resurrection heart and love to satisfy it. I have no patience with your transcendental, gelatinous, gaseous heaven.

II. The Place Where God Lives

What kind of a place will heaven be? For one thing it is where God, through Jesus, lives and rules. John wrote, "Now the dwelling place of God is with men, and He will live with them. They will be His people, and God Himself will be with them and be their God" (Rev. 21:3).

The word for *dwell* here is *tabernacle*. God is a spirit. He is not an old man with hands and feet and a face. God will live in heaven like He lived in the Old Testament tabernacle. He will let His glory shine there. This is why the Bible says, "They will not need the light of a lamp or the light of the sun, for the Lord God will shine on them" (Rev. 22:4).

Now we know it is absurd to say that God "lives" anywhere, because God lives everywhere. The Old Testament says, "The highest heaven cannot hold Him" (1 Kings 8:27). God lets part of His glory shine into heaven, and He lives there in and through Jesus Christ, the God-man.

When the Bible tells us we shall look upon God and see His face (Rev. 22:4), it is the face of God the Son, Jesus. He is "the image of the invisible God" (Col. 1:15). In Him, "all the fullness of the Godhead dwells" (Col. 1:19). He is the "radiance of God's glory" (Heb. 1:3). He is the One who said, "He who has seen me has seen the Father" (John 14:9).

As the disciples knew and saw and talked with Jesus, we too shall know and see and talk with Jesus. Tennyson said,

> Sunset and evening star
> And one clear call for me.
> And may there be no moaning of the bar
> When I put out to sea.
> For tho' from out our bourne of time and place,
> The flood may bear me far
> I hope to see my Pilot face to face
> When I have crossed the bar.[1]

III. A Place of Blessed Release

What kind of place is heaven for us? Words cannot explain it. No poet can describe it. Its blessedness and joy is beyond compare. As Dr. R. G. Lee stood by the grave of a young woman he had just buried, her little girl looked up and said, "Dr. Lee, what is heaven?" That grand old man of God said, "Heaven is the most beautiful and marvelous place that the wisdom of Christ could conceive and the power of Christ could compose." It is a place of joy (Ps. 16:11) where there is no suffering (Rev. 21:4) and no sin (Rev. 22:15).

The most beautiful sight I have ever seen is the Grand Canyon. But I agree with R. G. Lee when he says the Grand Canyon would be an ugly scar on the face of heaven. Let's look at the heaven where our loved ones are now and where we shall be one day with them, using the word *release*.

1. Heaven Is Release from Suffering (Rev. 21:4).

    Heaven is the blessed place of release from suffering. The Bible says, "He will wipe every tear from their eyes. There will be no more death or mourning or crying or pain, for the old order of things has passed away" (Rev. 21:4). This is not "pie in the sky" as our critics claim. It is the only thing that makes life make any sense.

    Why God asks some of His people to endure much suffering before they die, we do not know. All we know is that Jesus walked the same path. When people in pain cry out, "Where is God?" easy answers are an added blow. But we can say, "On the cross Jesus asked the same questions. He cried, 'My God! My God! Why hast Thou forsaken me?'" Alan Paton said, "Our Lord suffered. And I have come to believe that he suffered, not to save us from suffering, but to teach us how to bear suffering. For he knew that there is no life without suffering."

    The second thing we know is that God will put an end to the sufferer's pain. Heaven will heal us all. Heaven will dry every tear. Heaven will soothe every heart. The apostle Paul walked the valleys of pain. But when he thought of heaven he said, "For I consider that the sufferings of this present time are not worthy to be compared with the glory that is to be revealed to us" (Rom. 8:18). The poet says:

    > It is not death to die
    > To leave this weary road

> And midst the brotherhood on high
> To be at home with God.
> It is not death to close
> The eye long dimmed with tears
> To wake in glorious repose
> To spend eternal years.

I believe heaven is a blessing, not only to those who suffer, but to those who have had to watch their loved ones suffer. Even these tears will go. The great Methodist preacher W. E. Sangster's only sister never knew a day without pain for the nine years she lived. Fourteen operations and five gaping wounds in her head left her so disfigured that only the strong-nerved could look at her. Some looked and concluded, "There is no God," says Sangster. Others looked and offered shallow explanations. But Sangster says, "I was dumb as a boy and I am dumb as a man—I give to inquirers the answer which I gave to my school chums years ago, 'I'll wait till I get home and He'll tell me Himself.'"

> Not now but in the coming years
> It may be in the better land
> We'll read the meaning of our tears
> And there, sometime, we'll understand.

2. Heaven Is Release from Sin.

Heaven is also the blessed, joyful release from sin. The Bible says, "We shall be like Him (Jesus) for we shall see Him as He is" (1 John 3:2). The Bible says of heaven, "Nothing impure will ever enter it" (Rev. 21:27).

Down here we struggle with our lower nature and suffer the shame of giving in. Down here we are weak and even wicked. We hurt ourselves. We hurt those we love. We hurt our God. We say with Paul, "Oh wretched man that I am, who will rescue me" (Rom. 7:24). Our answer comes from the Christian martyr, who turned to his young friend as they were being led to the stake. He said, "Courage, brother, this fire will cure us both!"

3. Heaven Is Release from Separation.

Heaven is a community. It is a city. It is where God and His people live together. Thus, it is release from isolation and loneliness and separation. We are not separated from our Lord. Down here, we pray and search and grope and try to believe in the presence and love of God in our trials. Faith is often so hard to come by. How we long to see Jesus, to hear Jesus, and to reach out and touch Jesus, and to know that He is with us. Philip Yancey's new book calls this *reaching for the Invisible God*.

A young wife and mother died. The husband and his young son returned home from the funeral to brave the bitter grief of life without her. About midnight, as the dad lay in bed trying to sleep, he saw his little boy in the doorway.

"Daddy, I can't sleep. Can I get in the bed with you?" he said.

He got in and the two lay side by side in the darkness for a long time. The silence was broken.

The little boy's voice said, "Daddy, are you turned toward me?"

The dad said, "Yes!" and the little lad went to sleep.

In our darkness, we look up to the Heavenly Father and say, "Are you turned toward me?" We know He is, but it is often so hard to believe what we are supposed to know. But in heaven, all will be light, and the Bible says we will "see His face" (Rev. 22:4).

> Face to face with Christ my Savior
> Face to face what will it be
> When with rapture I behold Him
> Jesus Christ, who died for me.

In heaven we will not be separated from each other. We will be together in glory. There will be reunion. Abraham, Isaac, and Jacob met in heaven (Matt. 8:11). You, who have sent your loved ones across the great divide of death, will go to be with them.

The great slave preacher John Jasper got carried away in a sermon on heaven. He talked about rambling down the streets of glory and talking to Moses and David and Paul. And then he said, "And now I will ramble down the side streets to find the cabin in which the good Lord set up my mother in housekeeping. I will know it (He said) by the flowers in the garden and the vines on the cabin door."

There will be recognition in heaven. The resurrection of the body means we will be identifiable. People in heaven are called by their names. Jesus spoke of Abraham, Isaac and Jacob. Peter knew and recognized Elijah and Moses on the Mount of Transfiguration (Matt. 17:1–3). We are all different and special and unique. No two faces are alike. No two fingerprints are alike. No two people are alike. We are all identifiable. If we did not know each other in heaven, there would be no memory, and this earthly life would be a forgotten time and a tragic waste.

There will also be a mysterious revolution in our relationships. Jesus said, "The people of this age marry and are given in marriage. But those who are considered worthy of taking part in that age and in the resurrection from the dead will neither marry nor be given in marriage" (Luke 20:34–35).

One of the great mysteries is whether or not we will still bear the relationships such as fathers and sons or husbands and wives in heaven. I believe we shall remember these blessed relationships of earth, but in heaven, all will be new and better. I like the word *friend*. My wife will be my dear friend in heaven. My three children and I will be the closest of friends. My mother and I will be friends.

Finally, and best of all, there will be reconciliation. The idea of sitting at the table points to joyful communion. All the walls that divided us will be torn down. Sin will no more cloud our vision and cause division. When we lose loved ones, we all have regrets. But these will be healed in heaven's love. The old hymn said it well:

> We shall come with joy and gladness
> We shall gather round the throne
> Face to face with those that love us
> We shall know as we are known
> When the shadows have departed
> And the mists have rolled away
> We shall know as we are known
> Nevermore to walk alone
> In the dawning of the morning
> Of that bright and happy day
> We shall know each other better
> When the mists have rolled away.

4. Heaven Is Release for Service (Rev. 22:3).

Heaven is not, as some have pictured, a place of sterile, fruitless, boring inactivity where we lie around on clouds and do nothing but sing and go to church.

In Revelation 22:3 and 7:15, it is said we will "serve" God. Jesus talked of our being put in charge of cities (Luke 19:17 ff.), and Paul talked about our judging of angels (1 Cor. 6:3). Paul said in Ephesians 2:7 that in the ages to come God will show the riches of His grace to us. G. Campbell Morgan feels this may imply witnessing to other worlds in eternity.

We can only speculate as to what we will do, but we can rest assured we will do something. Henry Ward Beecher said, "After I am dead and people ask you where I am, tell them I am somewhere doing business for God."

The Hope of Heaven

It will be work, yes. But it will be work without weariness and boredom and frustration and failure and competition and pride and envy. The Bible promises that we will "rest from our labors" (Rev. 14:13). This great word *rest* does not mean we are asleep or inactive. It carries the meaning of being rested and refreshed and ready for the day's work with a song in our hearts. No one has pictured this better than this.

> When Earth's last picture is painted
> And the tubes are twisted and dried,
> When the oldest colours have faded
> And the youngest critic has died,
> We shall rest, and, faith, we shall need it,
> Lie down for an aeon or two,
> Till the Master of All Good Workmen
> Shall put us to work anew.
> And those that were good shall be happy;
> They shall sit in a golden chair;
> They shall splash at a ten-league canvas
> With brushes of comet's hair;
> They shall find real saints to draw from—
> Magdalene, Peter, and Paul;
> They shall work for an age at a sitting
> And never be tired at all!
> And only the Master shall praise us,
> And only the Master shall blame;
> And no one shall work for money,
> And no one shall work for fame,
> But each for the joy of the working,
> And each, in his separate star,
> Shall draw the Thing as he sees it
> For the God of Things as they are![2]

In your valley of grief, take your eyes off the scene of death. Do not dwell on the death bed. Lift your eyes to the heavenly scenes of life. Dwell upon that. The death scene is seen through the eyes of memory and is so real and painful. The heavenly scene is seen through the eyes of faith. What happens in you and to you and through you will depend upon your point of view. Do you see the one you love as dead or alive? As gone or arrived?

> Oh, say, "He has arrived!"
> And not that "He has gone."
> May every thought of him
> Be in that Land of Morn.
> Arrived! To hear His voice
> And see His welcoming smile;
> And then to greet again
> Those he has lost a while.
> Arrived! To tread no more
> The weary path of pain,
> Nor feel the waning strength
> The body feels, again.
> To be forever free
> From all that limits love,
> In joyful service thus
> He now may tireless move
> Then say not, "He has gone,"
> Nor think of him as dead;
> But say, "In the Father's House
> He has arrived"—instead.[3]

NOTES

[1] Alfred Tennyson, "Crossing the Bar," quoted in *The Funeral Encyclopedia: A Sourcebook*.
[2] Rudyard Kipling, "When Earth's Last Picture Is Painted" (New York City: Doubleday and Company, Incorporated).
[3] Author unknown, quoted in *The Funeral Encyclopedia: A Sourcebook*, 152, 153.

CHAPTER 5

For Those with No Miracle

This book will no doubt fall into the hands of some Christians who prayed earnestly for their loved one to be healed or spared from pain but received no healing miracle. When this happens, we often blame ourselves and are burdened with guilt. We blame God and are burdened with bitterness.

Because of the infiltration of the doctrines of charismatic Christianity, we have come to expect miracles as God's normal way of working. Reports of miraculous healings from so-called incurable diseases abound. God is pictured as One who always wants to heal if only we will have enough faith.

When our loved ones are not healed, we are bewildered. We are eaten alive by guilt. Did I not have enough faith? Was there something about me or my loved one that hindered the healing work of God? With bewilderment, there often comes bitterness. We who try and live for God with our imperfections wonder why others received God's healing touch and we didn't. We feel as though God is playing favorites and we are second-class citizens of His kingdom.

You may have read and believed all the prayer promises of Scripture, but no miracle came. You may have confessed all your sins and offered yourself as a substitute sacrifice, but no miracle came. You may have read and heard about thrilling accounts of others who were healed, but for you, no miracle came.

And today, deep within your soul, the greatest hurt is not the death or even the suffering of your loved one, but the fact that for you, no miracle came. God seems to have let you down. On the walls of a Georgia prison, one of life's walking wounded carved these words: "They ain't no God!" You know what he meant.

Suffering, especially unrelieved suffering in the face of prayer, is a "case" against either the power or the love of God. Sir Arthur Conan Doyle was an atheist. In his biography, he tells us that it was the horrible suffering he saw as a young doctor that drove him to lose any belief he had in a God of love.

He told of going to one very poor and dirty house. As he entered the tiny room, the mother motioned to a cot in the corner, and he knew the patient was there. Holding a candle, he went over, pulled back the sheet, and expected to see a child. What he saw was a malignant face with a pair of sullen brown eyes full of loathing and pain. What he saw was long, thin limbs twisted and coiled on the tiny couch.

Stepping away in horror, he asked the mother, "What is it?"

"It's a girl," she sobbed. "She's nineteen. Oh! If God would only take her!"

Things like this bother most of us. We are afraid to admit it, but they shake our faith. G. Studdert-Kennedy says the person who is undisturbed by the problem of pain suffers from either a hardening of the heart or a softening of the brain. To you who have walked this road, who have watched your loved ones waste away in pain, who have cried to God and received no miracle, I want to say three things that I hope will help.

I. God Does Not Explain Suffering

My first word is this: God does not explain suffering. Men do, but God does not! The Bible has a general theology of pain. We know suffering is one aftermath of the fall of Adam (Gen. 3:16–19). We know some people, like Herod (Acts 12:20–23), suffer because they are bad. Their pain is punishment. But we also know some people, like the Lord's apostles, James (Acts 12:2) and John (Rev. 1:9), suffer because they are good.

But who among us has the wisdom to tell any individual, this is why you suffer or this is why you were not healed? People with their smooth, shallow interpretations play God. But like Job's so-called friends, who had all the right answers, they are "miserable comforters" (Job. 16:2).

In his fine book *He Is Able*, Dr. W. E. Sangster tells about his little sister. Her nine years of life were spent almost totally in pain. Fourteen surgical invasions and five open wounds on her head left her with a marred face that only the strong could endure. Some, like Conan Doyle, looked and concluded, "There is no God." Sangster looked and had no answers but believed God would tell him why in the by and by. Worst of all, said Sangster, are those who look at her and others, like Conan Doyle, who saw and offer cheap and easy answers.

Can you imagine all these so-called Christians with their sunny view of healing encountering that little girl and her family or the girl and her mother in Conan Doyle's biography? Can you hear them prattle about the need only for faith as they suggest that God would heal the whole thing tomorrow if the loved ones would only believe and pray? To the burden of pain, they add the burden of guilt.

Can you imagine those who prop God up theologically as they prattle on about how we are all sinners who deserve worse than we get and that there is no such thing as undeserved suffering. I say, let such people walk through a children's ward and see the wires and tubes sticking in precious little ones. Let them listen to the unceasing screams of six-year-olds.

Can you imagine the supersaints telling these folks to "praise the Lord" and to "be thankful in everything and for everything." Now we know that the child of God, through the power of God, can learn to praise Him and find something to thank Him for in every situation. But this praise is like a river. The deeper it is, the quieter it is. There are some rare souls who can walk these valleys with a song on their lips. And we admire them.

But for most of us, this is a time for mute obedience. Here, silence is often golden. If we speak in our pain, we are often led to despair. If we speak in others' pain, we will probably treat their sorrow too lightly. If we endure pain, be assured that God still cares and will make it right someday. We are more than conquerors. The deepest faith often expresses itself not in words but in the upward look and the trustful silence and the faithful walk.

II. God Does Not Usually Heal Suffering

The Bible tells us that Jesus is "the same, yesterday, today, and forever" (Heb. 13:8). Because of the infection of charismatic doctrines we are led to interpret this to mean that just as Jesus healed all who came to Him, so will He heal all who come to Him today with enough faith. We are told that miracles are the order of the day. They are to be expected. When we don't get our miracle, we feel singled out. We feel guilty. We feel cheated. We feel unloved.

Certainly, God, in His character and in His ultimate purposes for men, is unchanging. He is the same yesterday, today, and forever. But God does change His methods. And in His dealings with man, He has chosen not to give an unbroken stream of healings and miracles.

In the Bible, there are only three periods where miracles were constant, where they were the "order of the day." The first was during the days of Moses. The second, the days of Elijah and Elisha. And the third was during the time of Jesus Christ and the early years of the apostles in the book of Acts. They were used by God to authenticate new eras in His dealings with man and the scriptures that were being written about those eras, the law (Moses), the prophets (Elijah), and the New Testament (Christ and the early apostles).

The vast majority of people in the vast majority of the Bible's time span lived without a constant flow of miracles. Men like Abraham, David, Jeremiah, and Hosea experienced miracles from time to time; but there were the exception and not the rule.

The question is, did all this change in the New Testament? Were the miracles of Christ and the apostles intended to stay throughout church history? The answer is, no! In the New Testament, we see the passing away of miracles after they served their purpose of bearing witness to the authenticity of the inspiration of New Testament Christianity.

The last recorded healing miracles in the New Testament were on the island of Malta (Acts 28:7–10). This was around AD 60. God, having introduced Christianity to the world, let them pass away, as He had always done. Paul, at first, healed the sick with his mere presence (Acts 19:11–12). But later, he couldn't even heal himself (2 Cor. 12:7–10) or those he loved like Timothy (1 Tim. 5:23) and Trophimus (2 Tim. 4:20). Paul was miraculously delivered from jail (Acts 16:16–28), but later, all he could do was ask for a coat to keep him warm (2 Tim. 4:13).

You ask, "But what about all these healings I hear about and see on TV?" A lot of it is fake, and most of it is simply sad misinformation. Dr. William A. Nolen, a fellow of the American College of Surgeons, chief of surgery at the Meeker County Hospital of Minnesota and on the board of editors of the Minnesota State Medical Journal, did an extensive study of the so-called healings of Kathryn Kuhlman. He examined eighty-two people who were "healed." Some, he found, were never really sick. Some thought they were healed, and later died of their disease. He did not find one single verifiable case of organic healing. He published his results in his book *Healing: A Doctor in Search of a Miracle*.

This is not to say that God never gives miraculous healing today. He does. He heals some through "faith healers," some through their own prayers, and some through the prayers of their Christian friends or their church. But this is the exception and not the rule. It was this way in Bible times. It has been this way throughout church history. It is this way today. God *is* the same, yesterday, today, and forever.

Why God grants healing in some cases and not in others, no one knows. It is hidden in the mystery of His sovereign ways and will. But it is simply not true that God heals us because we are dedicated or have faith. In fact, the opposite could often be true. God might let a person suffer and die to reveal his dedication and faith. And He might heal someone so they can have more time on earth to develop these virtues.

Paul spoke of the "fellowship of sharing in Christ's sufferings" (Phil. 3:10). The apostles rejoiced that they were counted worthy to suffer for the name of Christ (Acts 5:41). Charismatics teach that the faithful escape suffering. The Bible teaches that the faithful, like their Lord, endure suffering.

> And shall there be no cross for me
> In all this life of mine?
> Shall mine be all a flowery path
> And all the thorns be Thine?

The worst result of charismatic doctrine is that it often destroys the faith of God's good people. We watch our loved ones suffer and die in spite of our tears and prayers. We hear of all these others who are healed. And the result for many is a deadening agnosticism. We wonder if the One who created this universe cares anything about us. We are basing our faith upon the presence or absence of miraculous deliverance, and yet this is something God's word never tells us. In fact, we are told to expect and endure and seek relief only in heaven from sufferings and sorrow and trials. Paul said, "As servants of God we commend ourselves in every way; in great endurance; in troubles, hardships and distresses" (2 Cor. 6:4).

What does all this mean for you who received no miraculous cure? It means you have not been singled out for special punishment. It means you are not necessarily a second-class citizen of the kingdom. It means that your loved one's death was not the result of your lack of faith or goodness.

For reasons unknown to us, you simply traveled a road many take. A dreadful disease came, and as it does in the vast majority of cases, did not go away despite your piety and your prayers. This has been God's usual method with His people, in Bible history, and in church history. It is His method today.

The ones who have been singled out are those who received miraculous cures. As to the reason, we must leave that in the sovereign will of God. But we can be sure that it is not because they are His favorites or because they are better than the rest of us. Paul and Elisha and Stephen and Charles Spurgeon and Fanny Crosby and Helen Keller were not healed, and yet they rank at the very top of the kingdom. They, like the one you loved, could well have been choice souls, like Job, whom God could trust with trouble. Through them, God revealed to the devil and to the world that we love Him and believe in Him even when He doesn't put a protective wall around us (Job. 1:9–12).

III. God Does Use Suffering

Whatever we do not know about suffering, we do know that God uses it to make us better, stronger people. Paul prayed for God to remove his mysterious "thorn" (whatever it was). But God's answer was that He would not remove it, He would use it to make Paul stronger (2 Cor. 12:7–10). Even of Jesus, the Bible says, "He learned obedience through the things He suffered" (Heb. 5:8). Paul said, "We also rejoice in our sufferings, because we know that suffering produces perseverance; perseverance, character; and character, hope" (Rom. 5:3, 4).

One of the greatest sufferers of our generation and one recognized by many as the greatest character of our generation was Helen Keller. Miss Keller, deaf, dumb and blind, said, "In this world there is much suffering, and there is much overcoming of suffering."

If your loved one was called upon to suffer much physical pain, I want you to think not of their body, but of their spirit, their character, their inner courage. Of them, you can say:

> One by one their powers did depart,
> But courage sat smiling in their heart.

It is out of pain that some of life's sweetest juices are squeezed. In hospital rooms across our land, we see heroes both among those who suffer and those who minister to them. This little poem itself was found on a hospital wall:

> The cry of man's anguish went up to God;
> Lord, take away pain.
> The shadow that darkens the world
> Thou has made.

For Those with No Miracle

The close coiling chain
That strangles the heart;
The burdens that weigh
On the hearts that would soar.
Lord, take away pain
From the world Thou has made,
That it would love Thee more.
Then answered the Lord
To the cry of the world;
Shall I take away pain
And with it the power of the soul to
endure made strong by the strain?
Shall I take away pity
that knits heart to heart and sacrifice high?
Will ye love all your heroes that lift
from the fire white brows to the sky?
Shall I take away love that redeems with
a price and smiles at its loss?
Can you spare from your lives that would
climb into mine the Christ on His cross?
(Author Unknown)

POSTSCRIPT
(2018)

All the blessings found in this booklet are for those who are saved. If you have any doubts about this, stop right now, turn to God, and ask Him to forgive you on the basis of the cross where Jesus made forgiveness possible.

The book of Hebrews says the Old Testament sacrifices can be summed up in this: "Without the shedding of blood there is no forgiveness of sins" (9:22). On the night of His arrest, Jesus, in the Lord's Supper (Communion), lifted up the cup as a symbol and said, "This is my blood of the New Testament, shed for many for the forgiveness of sins" (Matt. 26).

We don't know why this had to be, and it seems Jesus wasn't sure because from the cross He asked why the Father had forsaken him (Matt. 27). The important thing is that He was willing to pay this price for you.

This is faith. This is turning to Jesus. When we turn to Jesus, we turn from a life we control to one He controls. We ask God to change us and help us live for Him. This is repentance. Put them together, and you have true conversion and true salvation.

> The people said, "What must we do?" And Peter said, "*Repent* and be baptized every one of you for the forgiveness of sins and you will receive the gift of the Holy Spirit (the new birth)—*Save yourselves* from this crooked generation." (Acts 2:37–38)

> *Repent* then and turn (*convert*) to God, so your sins can be wiped away. (Acts 3:19)
>
> *Believe* on the Lord Jesus Christ and you will be saved. (Acts 16:20)

I was in Sunday school all through my childhood years. I was baptized, and I believed Jesus died for me. Out of college and on my first job, I started thinking about a home and family, and from the people I met in church, I wanted a Christian home. I wanted a home not marked by conflict but by love.

I felt like I was a Christian, but I knew I was not living like it. I knew to find a Christian wife, I needed to get serious about living a Christian life. I ran my life and did what I wanted to. I felt, to make my decision real, I needed to make some kind of specific commitment; and for Baptists, that meant going forward in church.

By the side of my car one day, I looked up and asked Jesus to forgive me like He did those who crucified him, and I asked him to change me and help me live the way I should. This is what making a "commitment to live for Christ" talked about in this book means.

The first thing I did was buy a modern version of the Bible and start reading the New Testament through. When I came to John 3 and read where Jesus tells us to be "born again" if we want to go to heaven, I called my pastor and told him, I believe that when I "rededicated" my life, I was really converted—born again.

I had faith in Jesus, but I had not "repented," and in the New Testament, we must have both. We must remember that repentance *is willingness, not ability.* We don't have to "stop doing wrong things" to be saved. We can't lose weight, much less live like Jesus. For a year, I did not make a commitment because I knew I could never turn the other cheek (Matt 5–7), and I did not want to be a hypocrite and commit to something I knew I could not do.

A wise pastor told me he wasn't sure he could turn the other cheek. He said what God asks of us is to be willing to ask Him to help us be that kind of person.

Postscript

Telling people they have to stop some sins to be saved is like telling a child he cannot enter first grade until he can do algebra or quantum physics.

If we could do this with the right motives and attitudes and without pride, we would not need to be born again. Only God can help us stop doing wrong.

And this involves *growth*. Our heart (character) changes *instantly* in the new birth, and some changes can be seen in our life right away. But most of the changes come *gradually* over time. When I get angry, I cannot seem to help using profanity. So what I am asking God to do is help me learn how not to get angry.

If I get up to answer the phone in the middle of the night, stump my toe, fall, and break my television set, I might just use some profanity. But I would not, I could not go back to bed without asking God to forgive me and help me never do it again. This is what a true Christian is.

ABOUT THE AUTHOR

Rev. Bob Marcaurelle has been a Southern Baptist pastor for sixty-two years. His wife of fifty-seven years, Mary Ann, went home to heaven in 2022. They had three daughters, and they and their husbands presented them with six grandchildren. After retiring at age sixty-five, he formed a church in Anderson, South Carolina (Meadowbrook Baptist Church) that helps people who have come through hard times financially, as well as helping three other churches in the low-income areas. His hobbies are golf and writing. Since 1984, he has been furnishing printed sermons online, free, to pastors and missionaries all over the world. He is still preaching and pastoring at age eighty-six.